At the ... of the Moon

How the Moon Influences Your Mood, Your
Behaviour and Your Life

By:
Lori-ann Victoria Parker

PublishAmerica
Baltimore

First printing

At the specific preference of the author, PublishAmerica allowed this work to remain exactly as the author intended, verbatim, without editorial input.

ISBN: 1-4241-2769-6
PUBLISHED BY PUBLISHAMERICA, LLLP
www.publishamerica.com
Baltimore

Printed in the United States of America

Table of Contents

~Enter: the Moon~

Walk with me, friend, as a fellow inhabitant of this awe-inspiring Universal creation we call Planet Earth, while we explore the many wondrous and beautiful characteristics and personalities of the one we know as Luna. Let us examine the Moon's powerful, even magical influence on our lives, consider her role in ancient myths and legends, and investigate ways in which we can all tap into her interminable Mystical Power.

We will uncover new and ancient ways alike of using the Moon's influential forces in our every day life to achieve harmony with the universe and one another, for artistic power and vision as well as for our physical and mental well being. Come with me whilst I stroll about the Moon and endeavour to discern her Astonishing Beauty, unleash her Spellbinding Magic and open the portal to her Magnificent Power.

As well as being among the largest of the Celestial bodies in the Milky Way, the Moon is also the most magical and mysterious object in the night sky. If, by closely tracking her every move, we can determine what makes her such an extraordinary creature, we can in turn use this information to develop, strengthen and nurture our own inner Beauty and Power.

Because each one of us must follow the predestined path that is set out for us at the time of our birth, it is extremely important to be in touch with the hidden forces that shape our destiny. If we can somehow cease the struggle against the natural agreement of the Universe we can learn the valuable lessons that have to be learned and carry out that which needs to be accomplished in order to realize and develop our roles in this mysterious cycle we call Life.

When we recognise the remarkable impact and incredible power that the Moon has on this life, we will be better equipped to work *with* these forces rather than combating the natural structure of the Cosmos.

~Introducing Selena~

Perhaps because she is one of the most prevalent Celestial bodies in the Milky Way, the Moon remains the most extensively fabled Planet in Ancient Legend and Mythological Tale. Our Moon has been called by countless diverse names by different civilizations over the centuries. While the most well known of these names, Luna, came from the Ancient Romans, The Ancient Greeks as well had some time-honoured aliases for this lady. In Ancient Greece, the Moon was known by the popular designation Selena, but they also called her by such names as Artemis, the Divine Archer and Hecate, the Dark One.

The Moon was known to the peoples of Ancient Phyrgia by the majestic title of Cybele, the Lionesse. The Celts, as well called her by various mystical labels. The most renowned of these names was Cerridwyn, the Queen of the Cauldron and Danu, the Good Mother. While the Ancient Babylonians referred to her as Sinn, the peoples of Ancient China named their Moon Shing-Moo, and the Sumerians of old gave her the beautiful brand Lillith.

Khons, the Forgotten Egyptian was the title given our Lady of the night sky by the Ancient Egyptians. The Egyptians were also the people who so aptly named her Isis,

Mistress of the Magic. With whichever supernatural alias you choose to address her, The Moon will ever remain the most magnificent and splendorous body in the Heavens.

~From Whence She Came~

The moon is the only object in outer Space on which our unaided eyes can actually pick out features. When we are able to view an object in space without the use of a telescope, astronomers tell us that our eyes can *resolve features* on it. The Moon is bright enough to be seen easily by day, and her presence dominates our night sky.

Aside from being a spectacular sight to behold, what *practical* purpose does she serve to us here on Earth? Is the Moon simply an extraordinary ornament hanging in space for us to gaze at in awe and amazement? Or does she have a function in the great scheme of things? And how did she come to be? Who gave to us this gift? From whence came this globe full of mystery and wonder, eternally suspended from the ceiling of our world? It all started many, many lifetimes ago.

In the beginning, over four billion years ago, the Earth was covered in oceans, with land just poking through the waves. Complex molecules floated in the water, but the concentration of these particles wasn't high enough for them to evolve in to anything more than simple compounds.

Any depression in the rock would retain water that would not ebb away with the tide. Such tidal pools would collect the complex molecules, and as the water evaporated the concentration of these molecules would increase.

This as well increased the odds of progressively more complex molecules forming. After aeons and millennia the molecules were able to reproduce themselves, and take in energy in the form of sunlight or by absorbing other, less complicated molecules. When the tide returned, these living chains of atoms were swept into the ocean, where they could establish a foothold and begin their evolutionary journey of growth and development.

This process of molecules reproducing and evolving continued on for perhaps billions of years. Gradually, these once microscopic molecules began to form the starting point for what eventually became the Sun's amazing sister. Amazing though it may seem, those once infinitesimal building blocks of life have now evolved in to the most magnificent orb of luminescent splendour ever known to man, the Goddess of the Starry Sky, our Moon.

Although this theory does seem somewhat far-fetched given the utter compactness of a molecule and the contrasting sheer magnitude of the Moon, scientists today do believe this is how the Magnificent Mother Moon got her start in the Universe.

~Lunar Particulars~

The Moon is the only natural satellite of our breathtakingly beautiful planet, the Earth. The Moon's orbit is 384,400 kilometres from Earth. Her diameter is 3476 kilometres. And she has a mass of 7.35 kilograms.

Evidently, the Moon has been a well-known outpost to the inhabitants of planet Earth since prehistoric times. Not only is she a wondrous sight to behold, the Moon is also one of the biggest celestial beings in the Milky Way. Luna is the second largest object in the sky after the sun. Due to her size and composition, the Moon is sometimes classified as a "planet" along with the likes of Mercury, Venus, Mars, and of course, the Earth.

Unlike the Earth, however, the Moon has no atmosphere. Therefore there are no weather patterns on the Moon such as we experience here on Earth. For many years there had been some scientific evidence to suggest that there may be ice in some deep craters near the Moon's South Pole. These craters are permanently shaded from the sun and consequently remain very cold. There is apparently ice at the north pole of the Moon, as well.

The Moon has no global magnetic field of her own. But some of her surface rock however, exhibits a certain amount of remnant magnetism. This suggests to scientists that there may have been a global magnetic field early in the Moon's history.

With no atmosphere and no magnetic field, the Moon's surface is exposed directly to the solar wind. Hydrogen ions from the solar wind have become embedded in the dust on the Moon's surface.

Not only does the lack of atmosphere on the Moon prevent weather patterns from forming, but it also allows meteorites to fall on to it without being burned up by friction on their way down.

The Moon's crust, or regolith, averages 68 km thick. Below the crust, is the layer we refer to as the mantle. There has been a great deal of evidence to suggest that, similar to the Earth, there may also be a small core in the centre of the moon. Scientists believe this core is approximately 340 kilometres in radius. Unlike the Earth, however, the Moon's interior is no longer active. The centre of the Moon's mass is offset slightly from its geometric centre. Also, the crust of the Moon appears to be somewhat thinner on the near side.

There are two primary types of terrain on the Moon. These are the highlands and the mare. The highlands are heavily cratered and very old while the mare appears to be relatively smooth and a great deal younger. Comprising about 16% of the Moon's surface are huge impact craters that were later flooded by molten lava.

These craters are referred to as Maria. Most of the Moon's surface is covered with a mixture of fine dust and rocky debris produced by meteor impacts. This is called regolith.

For reasons not completely known to scientists as yet, the Maria are concentrated on the near side of the Moon's surface. The regolith, on the other hand, is concentrated mainly on the far side.

Craters are not strictly found on the near side of the Moon. She also boasts some huge craters on the far side. Some of them can be as big as 2250 km in diameter and 12 km deep. These craters form some of the largest impact basins in the entire solar system. The Lunar crust, as well also contains several multi-ring craters.

The Moon is the only Celestial body in the heavens that has ever been visited by spacecraft from Earth. The first Moon landing was on July 20, 1969 and the last was in December 1972. The Moon is also the only celestial being from which samples have been returned to Earth to study. In the summer of 1994, the Moon was mapped extensively by the spacecraft Clementine and again in 1999 by the Lunapar.

Many rock samples were returned to the Earth by the space craft on the Apollo mission. These samples provide us with most of our detailed knowledge of the Moon. Theses samples are particularly valuable because they can be dated. Most rocks on the surface of the Moon seem to be between 4.6 and 3 billion years old. This data provides scientists with evidence about the early history of the Solar System that is not available on the Earth.

Prior to the landing of the Apollo spacecraft on the Moon and the subsequent study of rock samples taken at that time, the origin of the Moon was a great mystery. While I am sure that the hypotheses and theories as to the origin of the moon are endless there are three principal theories. These ae the theories of Co-accretion, Fission and Capture.

The Co-accretion theory hypothesizes that the Moon and the Earth formed at the same time. Fissionists, on the other hand, theorize that the Moon split off of the Earth. While those that believe in the *capture* theory suggest that the Moon formed elsewhere and was subsequently captured by the Earth. In my opinion, none of these theories seem very realistic. However the new and much more in depth information from the Moon rocks led to the Impact theory. This theory holds that the Earth collided with a very large object and the ejected material from that collision formed what we now see as the Moon.

Due to its ever so slightly elliptical orbit, the Moon actually appears to rotate somewhat. This allows us to catch a brief glimpse of just a few degrees of the far side occasionally. Until the Soviet spacecraft Luna photographed it in 1959, the majority of the far side was a complete mystery to us here on Earth.

~Her Darker Side~

Although the Moon is the brightest object in the night sky, she doesn't emit any light of her own. From any location on the Earth, the Moon appears to be a circular disk that, at any specific time, is illuminated to some degree by direct sunlight. Like the Earth, the Moon is a sphere which is always half illuminated by the Sun, but as the Moon orbits the Earth we get to see more or less of the illuminated half.

The New Moon, as well is sometimes referred to as the Dark Moon. This is because at the time of the New Moon it is completely invisible to us here on Earth. Thus being invisible for a few days, some people called her the Dark Moon.

Although scores of folktales and songs from long ago tell of a mysterious "Dark Side" of the moon, it does not actually exist. There is no **one** side of the moon that remains dark all of the time. With the exception of a few deep craters near the pole, all parts of the Moon get sunlight half the time. Some uses of the term "dark side" in the past may have referred to the far side as the "dark side" simply because it was so mysterious.

Lunar Meteorites

As their name quite plainly suggests, Lunar meteorites, or lunaites, are meteorites from the Moon. This simply means that they are rocks found on Earth that were ejected from the Moon by the impact of an asteroidal meteorite.

The speed at which an object must travel in order to be projected off the Moon is called "Lunar Escape Velocity". This speed is 2.38 kilometres per second or 1.48 miles per second. Any rock accelerated by an impact on the surface of the moon to "lunar escape velocity" or faster will leave the Moon's gravitational influence. When this happens, some of this matter may become captured by the Earth's gravitational field. This causes the object to land on Earth after ejection from the Moon.

Some of the other ejected matter ends up in orbit around the Sun. While this material may hit the Earth, eventually as well, it could take an eternity to do so. One Lunar Meteorite called Yamato remained in space for about 9 million years before it finally landed on the Earth somewhere in Antarctica.

Just like Asteroidal meteorites, lunar meteorites have fusion crusts from the melting that occurs as they enter the Earth's atmosphere.

As well, they are comprised of certain isotopes that can only be produced by reactions with cosmic rays while outside the Earth's atmosphere.

At this point, you may be wondering just how Scientists know for sure whether the material they found actually comes from the Moon. During the Apollo expeditions, samples of the Moon were collected and brought back to earth for analysis. The chemical compositions, isotope ratios, minerals, and textures of the Lunar meteorites are all similar to those of the samples collected on the Moon by the Apollo astronauts.

These characteristics vary a great deal from any other type of meteorite or terrestrial rock. For example, all of those meteorites that are classified as feldspathic breccias are rich in the mineral anorthite. These meteorites all have high concentrations of aluminium and calcium. Because of some unique aspects of the formation of the Moon, the lunar highlands are composed predominantly of Anorthite. This mineral is much less common on asteroids. As far as we know to date, Anorthite is not found on the surface of any other celestial body.

At the present time, approximately 42 Lunar meteorites have been found and recorded in scientific accounts. Meteorites themselves are very rare rocks and Lunar meteorites are exceedingly so.

Although the discovery of Meteorites from the Moon is relatively new, lunar rocks have certainly been landing on the Earth for an eternity. Lunar Meteorites are not always easy to find or to recognize, though. Many times, a Lunar Meteorite is passed by because of its close resemblance to the types of rocks we regularly see on Earth.

The concentration of iron or aluminium is a useful way to identify and classify Lunar rocks. While Meteorites from one part of the Moon, the Mare, are low in aluminium and rich in iron, Meteorites from the other part, the Feldspathic Highlands are rich in aluminium and poor in iron. As well, most locations on the lunar surface are Very low in radioactivity and such is the case with most of the meteorites that are believed to have been from the Moon.

Most of the lunar meteorites are composed of fine material from near the surface of the Moon. Studying this material helps to provide us with a better estimate of the composition and mineralogy of the crust of the Moon than we were able to obtain from the samples taken during the Appolo Expedition.

~She Orbits, She Eclipses~

As the Moon orbits around the Earth, once per month, the angle between the Earth, the Moon and the Sun constantly changes. This change can be witnessed from Earth with the naked eye as the cycle of the Moon's phases. The time between successive new moons is 29.5 days.

This is slightly different from the Moon's orbital period which is measured against the stars since the Earth moves a significant distance in its orbit around the Sun in that time. The cycle of the Moon's phases causes great changes on our planet, the Earth and in the people that inhabit it.

Eclipses of the Moon occur when She is in between the Earth and the Sun. This type of eclipse occurs only when the moon is full. Each year we are able to witness three or four eclipses of this type. Most of them are partial eclipses which can last for about an hour. Whereas a total eclipse usually only lasts for a few minutes.

The Lunar Eclipse

A lunar eclipse occurs when the Earth lies between the Sun and the Moon, so that Earth's shadow darkens the Moon. This can only happen at full Moon. The dark, central shadow is the *umbra,* while the lighter shadow that surrounds the umbra is the *penumbra.* The penumbral shadow is difficult to detect; for most observers a lunar eclipse really starts when the umbra first touches the lunar surface. When the Moon is completely immersed in the Earth's umbral shadow we call it totality.

Lunar eclipses get their colourful red-orange hues from

sunlight that is filtered and bent by the Earth's atmosphere before it reaches the Moon. Intense and colourful eclipses take place when our planet's upper atmosphere is transparent. Major volcanic eruptions that spew dust and aerosols skyward often result in darker lunar eclipses. The Moon's brightness varies greatly from eclipse to eclipse, which would tell a lot about the state of the Earth's upper atmosphere if only we understood it better

The Solar Eclipse

A Solar Eclipse occurs when the moon gets in the way of the sun as seen from the planet Earth.

There is an amazing cosmic coincidence that the Moon is about 400 times closer to the Earth than the Sun. At the same time, the Sun is about 400 times larger than the Moon.

What this means is that the size of the Sun and Moon as seen from the surface of the Earth is about the same in the sky. When viewed from the surface of Earth, both the moon and sun appear to be about **one** half degree in size. One half degree is about the size of your thumbnail in relation to your entire arm.

In astronomical terms, the Sun and Moon have roughly the same angular **size**. This makes it possible for a solar eclipse to occur. No other planets in our solar system enjoy the same one-to-one ratio.

A solar eclipse can only occur during a "New Moon" phase. At that time the Moon lies between the Earth and Sun thus projecting a shadow back towards the Earth. During a Full Moon, when the moon is at the opposite side of its orbit, a lunar eclipse can occur. During a lunar eclipse the surface brightness of the full moon drops considerably. The light refracting through the Earth's atmosphere causes the moon to change colours, somewhat. At this time, the Moon appears to be a glowing crimson colour. Although this type of eclipse is not quite as spectacular as a total solar eclipse, it is still an awesome sight to behold.

Light traveling from the top and bottom of the sun travels

in straight lines. In fact, light is coming from all points on the sun in straight lines, but we only consider the top and bottom points. Tracing lines that also hit the edge of the "red ball" we can see how this cone is formed. There is a "dark" area where light from the top and bottom do not shine around the ball. This dark area is called the Umbra shadow. Around the umbra shadow is a lesser shadow where only a portion of the light is blocked. This is called the Penumbra shadow.

In order to have the entire bright surface of the sun covered, you must be in the Umbra shadow. Only in the umbra shadow is all light of the sun's bright surface blocked. At that time, during the total solar eclipse, you can look directly at the sun and behold other features of our day-star. At all other times, a solar filter is required.

~Harnessing Her Magic~

Let's consider for a moment all the power that the Sun and the Moon possess and emit. Wouldn't it be terrific if we could find some way to tap into and use the power of the Moon in the same way as we use Solar power? Well, the fact is, we have the technology to be able to do just that. It is feasible that Lunar power could provide a clean, emission-free, and unlimited source of energy. Lunar energy called Power beams could supply all the needs of the entire world in the 21st century and beyond.

David Criswell, a physicist and Space Age veteran says

"We think of beaming power from the moon as exotic, but it has been done for at least 15 years. Power beaming is like using a big radar."

David Criswell is the director of the Institute for Space Systems Operations at the University of Houston. He began examination of lunar-based power systems more than 20 years ago. During that time he worked at the Lunar Science Institute which we now call the Lunar and Planetary Institute.

He proposes a Lunar Solar Power System (LSP), using lunar materials to build bases on the moon to collect solar energy. Much like solar panels we use on Earth today, these bases collect lunar energy and convert it to microwaves. These microwaves would then be beamed to thousands of receivers around the Earth. The microwaves would then be converted into electricity to be fed into local power grids.

Although this sounds a bit like an excerpt from a Sci-Fi novel the fact is that successful Earth-moon power beams are already in use today. A radio telescope operating from the Arecibo Observatory in Puerto Rico regularly uses a beam of microwaves to produce images of the moon.

The proposed LSP System would consist of between 20 and 40 power bases located on the eastern and western edge of the moon. Criswell estimates that in 2050, a world population of about 10 billion people would require about 20 terawatts of power. The moon receives more than 13,000 terawatts of solar power, and harnessing just one percent could satisfy Earth's power needs.

One of the drawbacks of this project is the tremendous financial expense. And although it is technically feasible, it remains unlikely at this time not only because of the cost, but also because astronauts haven't been to the Moon in 30 years. Some researchers worry that scientists and astronauts don't have a concise idea of how to utilize the moon's powerful resources. Because of the lack of funding and a possible lack of experience on the Moon this project may have to be temporarily put on hold. However, technically this project is ready willing and able to fly should it ever get off the ground.

~What Are Nodes?~

As you know, the Moon makes a monthly voyage around the Earth. As the Earth revolves around the Sun, the Moon has to cross this orbit of the Earth twice during each month.

At one time, it goes to the North of it and the other time it goes to the South. The first crossing of the Moon has been named the North Node and the South node is the name that has been given to its return voyage.

The Moons nodes are sometimes called by various other names. The North Node is sometimes called the Dragon's Head or Caput. By contrast, the South Node is often penned Cauda or the Dragon's Tail. The function of the Nodes of the Moon is to cause light to focalize at the North Node and to cause it to scatter at the South Node. The influence of the North and South Nodes with respect to where they were on a person's date of birth can give us many hints about our life and personalities.

If the South Node was predominant at the time of your birth, it seems to spread its influence. A great number of people or events will be affected. This is also the area of the moon that gives one the resources he needs to give of himself. It may also be where there is a Karmic debt to pay.

{NOTE**The Sanskrit meaning of Karma is an Act, a Deed or Work.}**

This seems to be the point that indicates our destiny. Each of us is born during a certain lunar cycle to carry out a certain action or fulfil a certain Karmic predestination. Whatever you choose to call it, the point is that each one of us is required to learn a lesson or to atone for something and we can only do that if the time is right for us. The right time occurs only within a certain period in time.

At the North Node, there seems to be somewhat of shyness, at first. It is where we learn to take in events and information. Eventually, as the South Node proceeds throughout a person's life, with its teaching and giving, the necessary lesson will be learned. Either that, or the Karma will be paid. Then success is achieved and the process can be balanced. When the moon crosses the Nodes it can cause certain things to happen in your life.

You may suddenly feel an intense desire to redecorate your house or maybe even move to a new one altogether. You might feel like going on vacation to a destination completely different from anywhere you've been in the past.

The moon crossing the Nodes can also cause interesting things like out of the ordinary visitors dropping by unannounced. As well you may feel the need to entirely reappraise the direction your life is taking during this time.

With all this being said, you may be wondering what impact, if any, all of this has on your life, as an individual. If we take in to consideration the
concept of time, the whole thing is a little easier to understand. Time, you see is not a firm concept . On the contrary; it is quite difficult to understand and to pin down. All of us here on Earth, however, are bound by it for eternity. We are taken forward in motion on this planet and to the next plane, whether we wish to be or not.

Since none of us possess the ability to make time stand still, our job as inhabitants of the Earth is to learn how to flow with it rather than to fight it. To fight against time is a waste of our energy. Our resistance only weakens our attempt to move forward.

By not fighting the natural structure of things we can learn what needs to be learned and accomplish what we must in order to grow and discover our roles in this mysterious cycle we call life.

When we recognise the impact and the power that the Moon as well as many other unseen forces has on our life we will be that much better able to work with these forces rather than fighting the natural structure of the Universe.

~No Quarter~

During each lunar orbit of approximately one month, we here on Earth can watch the appearance of the Moon go from dark through partially illuminated to fully illuminated, then back through partially illuminated and back to dark again. Although this cycle is a continuous process, there are eight distinct, traditionally recognized stages, called phases.

The phases designate both the degree to which the Moon is illuminated and the geometric appearance of the illuminated part. These phases of the Moon, in the sequence of their occurrence (starting from New Moon), are listed following .

New Moon - The Moon's "dark" side is facing the Earth. The Moon is not visible (except during a solar eclipse).

Waxing Crescent - The Moon appears to be partly but less than one-half illuminated by direct sunlight. The fraction of the Moon's disk that is illuminated is increasing.

First Quarter - One-half of the Moon appears to be illuminated by direct sunlight. The fraction of the Moon's disk that is illuminated is increasing.

Waxing Gibbous - The Moon appears to be more than one-half but not fully illuminated by direct sunlight. The fraction of the Moon's disk that is illuminated is increasing.

Full Moon - The Moon's illuminated side is facing the Earth. The Moon appears to be completely illuminated by direct sunlight.

Waning Gibbous - The Moon appears to be more than one-half but not fully illuminated by direct sunlight. The fraction of the Moon's disk that is illuminated is decreasing.

Last Quarter - One-half of the Moon appears to be illuminated by direct sunlight. The fraction of the Moon's disk that is illuminated is decreasing.

Waning Crescent - The Moon appears to be partly but less than one-half illuminated by direct sunlight. The fraction of the Moon's disk that is illuminated is decreasing.

~Lillith Crescent, Gibbous~

Following the waning crescent is the New Moon which begins a repetition of the complete phase cycle of 29.5 days. The time in days counted from the time of New Moon is called the Moon's "age". Each complete cycle of phases is called a "lunation".

Because the cycle of the phases is shorter than most calendar months, the phase of the Moon at the very beginning of the month usually repeats at the very end of the month. When there are two Full Moons in a month (which occurs, on average, every 2.7 years), the second one is called a "Blue Moon". So the next time you hear someone express "...once in a Blue Moon..." you'll know more of how that saying evolved.

Although Full Moon occurs each month at a specific date and time, the Moon's disk may appear to be full for several nights in a row if the sky is clear. This is because the percentage of the Moon's disk that appears illuminated changes very slowly around the time of Full Moon. This also occurs around New Moon, but the Moon is not visible at all then.

The Moon may appear 100% illuminated only on the night closest to the time of exact Full Moon, but on the night before and night after will appear 97-99% illuminated. Most people would not notice the difference with the naked eye alone. Even two days from Full Moon the Moon's disk is 93-97% illuminated, so it may still appear to be full to some onlookers.

The New Moon, First Quarter, Full Moon, and Last

Quarter phases are considered to be primary phases. Their dates and times are published in almanacs and on calendars.

The two crescent and two gibbous phases are intermediate phases. Each of these phases lasts for about a week between the primary phases. During this time the exact fraction of the Moon's disk that is illuminated gradually changes.

The phases of the Moon are related to and actually caused by the relative positions of the Moon and Sun in the sky. For example, New Moon occurs when the Sun and Moon are quite close together in the sky. Full Moon occurs when the Sun and Moon are at nearly opposite positions in the sky. This explains why a Full Moon rises about the time of sunset, and sets about the time of sunrise, in most locations on Earth.

The First and Last Quarters occur when the Sun and Moon are about 90 degrees apart in the sky. In fact, the two "half Moon" phases are called First Quarter and Last Quarter because they occur when the Moon is, respectively, one- and three-quarters of the way along its orbit of the sky from the New Moon.

~From Candle Moon to Blood Moon~

The following is a completed lunar calendar for this year. I have included a brief paragraph about the common associations for each lunar month along with the approximate dates of the celestial events and Quarter and Cross-Quarter celebrations in each lunar month.

This Calendar follows the pagan tradition which holds

that the old year ends with the descent of the solar deity into the underworld on October 31st which then plunges the world above into the darkness of winter. The first moon of our new year, then, is the first new moon appearing after the complete moon phase that contains October 31st.

This calendar perfectly illustrates that 13 full lunar cycles may not begin and end on the same days which mark the beginning and ending of the year. For the lunar year in this example, the new pagan year (11-1) begins while still under the influence of the last moon-phase of the old year and ends while only halfway through the final moon-phase of the current year (10-31).

So, the 13 lunar cycles for the year are all represented, but the 13th cycle contains the both the end of the old year, and the beginning of the new year and a whole new cycle. Doesn't it seem like this is precisely the way it should be? This seems nothing short of logical to me, as the word cycle is a synonym for circle and a circle has no beginning and no ending.

The following shows approximate dates for the given names of the Moon phase based on the 2003 Calendar. To get a more accurate date for this year, simply check a current calendar.

The Candle Moon (a time for divination)
Quickening energy, Beginning and conceiving, Awakening compassion, Looking to the future and its needs.
2-1-03* Candle Moon - **New**
2-2-03* Candlemas, Imbolc, Festical of Lights, (Awakening)
2-16-03* Candle Moon- **Full**
2-21-03* **Pisces** Rises

The Maiden Moon (a time for awakening)

The first cry of energy breaking the veil of illusion. A balance of light against dark. Fire withstands ice. Making way for new beginnings, growth, discovery and prosperity.

3-3-03 Maiden Moon - **New**
3-18-03 Maiden Moon - **Full**
3-21-03 **Aries** Rises
3-21/22/23-03 O stara, Eostar, Spring Equinox, (The Meeting)

The Seed Moon (a time for growth)
Creative energy flows from the growth of all things. Strengthened connections to all powers natural and supernatural. Radience illuminates your path.

4-1-03 Seed Moon - **New**
4-6-03 Daylight Savings Time Changes
4-16-03 Seed Moon - **Full**
4-20-03 **Taurus** Rises

The Honey Moon (a time for love)
Full peaceful energy protects, strengthens, and wards the future. Romance, beauty, and healing are revealed in this light.

5-1-03 Honey Moon - **New**
5-1-03 Beltane, Mayday, WhiteSun, (The Marriage)
5-16-03 HonetyMoon**Full**
5-21-03 **Gemini** Rises

The Blessing Moon (a time for magic)
Energy moves into creation. Opportunities for self-reliance and confidence bloom. Unity and balance.

5-31-03 Blessing Moon - **New**
6-14-03 Blessing Moon - **Full**
6-21/22/23-03 Litha, Midsummer, Summer Solstice, (Maturity)
6-22-03 **Cancer** Rises
The Mystery Moon (a sacred time)

Secrets are guarded in darkness. The spiritual alchemy of life, death, and rebirth are the earth tides turning within the wheel of life.

6-29-03 Mystery Moon - **New**
7-13-03 Mystery Moon - **Full**
7-23-03 **Leo** Rises

The Harvest Moon (a gathering time)
Energy achieving fullness and success. A good time for dream work, meditation, divination, and preparation for the spiritual harvest which will sustain life.

7-29-03 Harvest Moon - **New**
8-1-03 Lammas, Lughnasadh, Harvest Home, (The Decline)
8-12-03 Harvest Moon - **Full**
8-23-02 **Virgo** Rises

The Singing Moon (a time for exhilaration)
Completion, acceptance, mellowing, and rest after labour. A balance of light and dark lead to organization and clean-up of physical, mental, emotional, and spiritual clutter.

8-27-03 Singing Moon - **New**
9-10-03 Singing Moon - **Full**
9-21/22/23-03 Mabon, Autumn Equinox, Winter Finding, (Croning)
9-23-03 **Libra** Rises

Blood Moon(a time for sacrifice)
Letting go and clearing away to find justice, balance, and harmony. Inner cleansing and the lament of loss. Seeking shelter in friendship, karma, and reincarnation.

10-25-03 Blood Moon- **New**
10-26-03 Daylight Savings Time Changes ***10-31-03*** Samhain, Shadowfest, All Hallows Eve, (The Death)
11-1-03 The New Lunar Year Begins
11-9-03 Blood Moon – **Full**
Full Hot Moon

Certain cultures and civilizations have different names for each month of the year. Following are just some of the names given to what we call January, February and March.

Names	Month	Her Aliases
Full Wolf Moon	**January**	Full Old Moon
Full Snow Moon	**February**	Full Hunger Moon
Full Worm Moon	**March**	Full Crow Moon, Full Crust Moon, Full Sugar Moon, Full Sap Moon
Full Pink Moon	**April**	Full Sprouting Grass Moon, Full Egg Moon, Full Fish Moon
Full Flower Moon	**May**	Full Corn Planting Moon, Full Milk Moon
Full Strawberry Moon	**June**	Full Rose Moon, Full Hot Moon
Full Buck Moon	**July**	Full Thunder Moon, Full Hay Moon
Full Sturgeon Moon	**August**	Full Red Moon, Full Green Corn Moon
Full Harvest Moon*	**September**	Full Corn Moon, Full Barley Moon
Full Hunter's Moon	**October**	Full Travel Moon, Full Dying Grass Moon
Full Beaver Moon	**November**	Full Frost Moon
Full Cold Moon	**December**	Full Long Nights Moon

Note the harvest moon is usually the first full moon after the equinox.

~Queen of the Cauldron Calendar~

Both the Sun and the Moon have been synonymous with certain attributes ever since the dawn of time. The Moon, however, was the first universal measurer of time. In fact, in our culture, the Moon has come to symbolize time, fate, the wheel, and of course the Great Mother or Feminine influence.

The peoples of ancient cultures showed a consideration of time much different than we view it today. They treated it like a circle with no beginning and no ending. Since most people lived off the land it was imperative they knew the cycles and the laws of Mother Nature to ensure their survival and prosperity. They observed their surroundings meticulously and concluded that the various phases of the moon coincided with environmental events and situations. This enabled them to learn to plant, fish, harvest, hunt, and make predictions, all by the light of the silvery moon.

The cycles of the heavens are symbolized in the various ways all throughout our life here on Earth. The American Indian Tribes use a Medicine Wheel as their symbol of life everlasting. The Egyptian's have what they refer to as the Wheel of the Law to symbolize the great journey and the Tibetan's refer to a Prayer Wheel. The Moon is an integral part of each of these life-models. In Astrology, the Moon is sometimes said to symbolize the horoscope itself.

Astronomical calendars are based on the rotation of the Earth (the day), the revolution of the Earth around the Sun (the year), and the revolution of the Moon around the Earth (the month). The concepts would be much easier to grasp if all these cycles were synchronized. Unfortunately they do not quite agree.

Out of this failure to harmonize, three distinct calendars have arisen. Because of the complexity of the lunar cycles and to keep step with the seasons, three distinct types of calendars developed

We have the Solar calendar, the Lunar calendar and the lunar-solar or Solunar calendar. The West's Gregorian calendar is a prime example of a Solar calendar. It is based on the tropical year. Every fourth year is a leap year in which an extra day is added to keep synchronicity. The lunar calendar follows the phases of the moon instead of the seasonal or tropical year. The Solunar calendar follows the lunar cycle but has a13th month intercalated to bring the calendar back in phase with the tropical year.

The Islamic calendar is an example of a purely lunar cycle. Over a period of about thirty-three years, the months slowly regress through the seasons. Each month begins with the first sliver of the waxing Moon, although for civil purposes a tabulated calendar is used that approximates the lunar cycle. The mean length of the month on the civil calendar is only 2.9 seconds less the than synodic cycle.

There are "Man made" lunar calendars that some scientists place as old as 32,000 years. Some recent archaeological findings are from the Ice Age where hunters carved notches and gouged holes into sticks, reindeer bones and the tusks of mammoths, depicting the days between each phase of the Moon. These artefacts are dated between 25,000 and 10,000 B.C. There are also surviving astronomical records inscribed on oracle bones dating back to the Shang dynasty of the fourteenth century B.C. that reveal a Chinese calendar, with intercalation of lunar months.

In Egypt, the paths of the stars were recorded as early as 6,000 years before Christ. The wisest of the Egyptians were the Hermetic philosophers, who possessed a profound knowledge of the sky. They relied upon the predictable motion of these bodies through the sky to determine the seasons, months, and years. People began a preoccupation with measuring and recording the passage of time. There was a need for planning and for divination and prognostication; to maintain these cycles meant that records needed to be kept and observatories needed to be built to precisely measure these cycles.

They erected various calendars to provide a source of order and cultural identity and as a need to organize their time more efficiently. As far back as 5,000 to 6,000 years ago civilizations in the Middle East and North Africa also made primitive clocks in order to divide their time more precisely. Of primary importance to the Egyptians was the time when the Nile River began its annual flood tide. This was carefully noted so they knew when to plant and harvest.

All of their activities, whether for work, rest or play were in harmony with the flow of "Mother Nature," the changing of seasons, the rising and setting of the Sun and Moon and the phases the Moon passed through in a month. There was a time for everything under the Heavens! The seasons, tides eclipses and phases of the Moon were known to be in direct correlation to the movement of the Sun, Moon, and Earth.

In ancient times, much like it is today, people realized they had little or no control over the laws of nature. The ebb and flow of the seasons and coming of different weather patterns were seen as a mysterious turning of the great wheel of life. Again like us today, they were honoured to be a part of such a great and wondrous affair. Studying these observations also meant that precise measurements needed to be kept and observatories needed to be established to measure these cycles. These observations formed the universal laws that are the foundations of ancient wisdom. As above, so below.

~Your Moon Sign Shapes You~

During each lunar orbit which takes one lunar month, we

see the Moon's appearance gradually and cyclically change. These visible changes are what we term the Phases of the Moon. Many cultures believe that the Phases of the Moon contain powerful hidden forces that impact us here on Earth. The Moon phases control everything around us including our behaviour and our mood. To find out what phase the Moon was in when you were born, consult a good Astrologer if you know one, if not an Ephemeris will do.

If you were born during the First Quarter:

You will have an underlying sense of youthful enthusiasm. You may prefer to take the first step in romance. You will always be ready to look for new interests in life. You have a lively outlook on life, but you will need to be careful not to be selfish. You may be a real go-getter who sometimes has trouble seeing a task through completion. It is likely that you will be self employed. Depending on other factors in your life, you should get off to a good start and become quite successful while you are still fairly young. You would be wise to think things through carefully before you act or react and try not to take others by surprise.

If you were born during the Second Quarter:

You are likely a very sociable and ambitious person. You feel a strong need to have a place of your own where you can express your self. You have a magnetic personality that will always draw others toward you. You try to be helpful to others as much as you can but sometimes find it hard to make any personal sacrifices. Although you may tend to use others for your own benefit or gain, this behaviour is instinctive rather than calculated. You need to draw attention to yourself and this can cause you to sometimes be insensitive to the needs of others. You are usually slow to anger, but once you reach the boiling point, look out world! Although you do not like to be hurried your self, you do not

AT THE FEET OF THE MOON

mind hurrying others if it keeps them slightly off-balance and consequently tipping their odds in your favour.

If you were born during the Third Quarter:

Because you are highly sensitive to the needs of others, you would like them and sometimes expect them to be sensitive to yours. You need friendships and relationships and work very well in a group setting. You enjoy an exciting life but need others to share it with. You are somewhat concerned with other's opinions of you and consequently you may not be entirely sure of yourself unless you get acceptance from other people. Although it is likely that you will be an overachiever, you will always need the company and encouragement of others to make you feel at ease. Because you are full of nervous energy and possess a quick wit and a somewhat short attention span you will remain on an endless search for new and exciting things.

Sex may be of special significance to you and may transform your life in some way. It is said that people born on the third quarter, just after the Full Moon has passed the mid haven will be rich and famous. The most successful time in your life will be your mid-life.

If you were born during the Fourth Quarter:

You tend to find yourself finishing projects that others have started. As well you may find that you regularly reorganize and sort out other peoples problems. You have tremendous intuitive insight and may follow your hunches rather than work through things logically. You may be inclined to sit back and let things just happen around you. You have the ability to either blend in with a large group or work entirely on your own. Although you do need a certain amount of job satisfaction, you are not a materialistic person. Though you may be slow to grow up, once you do, you will go through some sort of change or metamorphosis later in life. Once this happens, you will achieve great success in something unusual and totally individual.

Born on a Luna Eclipsa?

If the Moon was lying in between the Earth and the Sun when you were born, your inner and outer personalities will interact well. Your emotional reactions will be fast and you will be able to act instinctively. This will help you to avoid sticky situations or get out of them if the need arises. This might also make it hard for you to make plans and carry them through to fruition.

If the Sun was between the Earth and the Moon when you were born, you will be restless, intense, and highly creative. You may find yourself going overboard in your relationships because of your tendency to take everything very seriously.

You need to have people around you so it is good you possess the ability to draw them near to you. If you allow your logic to over ride your instincts, you may end up misjudging situations where it would have been important to trust your gut reaction.

~Full Moon Fever?
Or Simply a Scapegoat~

Do you think the full moon has some unexplainable effect on our behaviour? Early psychologists had no doubt about the moon's effect on our mental states. The "lunatic," (derived from the Latin "Luna" or moon) was separated from the chronically nature insane, and extra staff was called into the asylums on the full moon. Special allowances were often made before the full moon.

**In 1983 there was a study done on poison control

centres. This study found that unintentional poisonings actually increased on the Full Moon. The same study found that suicide attempts and drug overdoses increased on the New Moon.

**In 1991 a study on women who were developmentally delayed found that these women misbehaved more on a Full Moon.

** A study of the Emergency Rooms of several American Suburban Hospitals found nobody was admitted for howling at the Full Moon.

The same study found identical results on the New Moon

**A study of absenteeism in the work place found that more people show up for work on a Full Moon.

**Another study revealed that people seemed to eat larger meals on a Full Moon by at least eight percent.

That same study found that people consumed less alcohol on full Moon days, with the New Moon showing an increase of alcohol consumption.

**The English labourer Charles Hyde was acquitted on murder charges on the grounds that he was under the spell of the full moon.

**The American Institute for Climatology concluded, psychotic crimes such as arson, kleptomania, dangerous driving, and homicidal alcoholism, all increased on a Full Moon.

The study found, as well that cloudy nights offered no protection against this trend.

The December 23, 2000 issue of the *British Medical Journal* answered the question of whether animals bite people more during a full moon. Chanchall, Bhattacharjee and colleagues at the Bradford Royal Infirmary in Bradford, England, reviewed 1,621 patients admitted to the infirmary's emergency room between 1997 and 1999 for animal bites and found that the chances of being bitten were twice as high on or around full-moon days. Sounds like a case of Full Moon Fever, to me.

So, whether you believe in Full Moon Fever or not, the research certainly seems to suggest that the phase of the Moon, be it a Full Moon or a New Moon does have a perceptible affect on people's behaviour.

~Put the Blame on Gravity~

Although the jury is still out on the subject, there is substantial evidence to suggest that the full moon does have a substantial affect on our behaviour and our disposition. One theory behind this alleges that it is the gravitational pull on the earth and its inhabitants that causes such drastic and sometimes unspeakable changes in humans.

While this theory remains to be proven beyond a shadow of a doubt, it is true that the gravitational forces between the Earth and the Moon do cause some interesting effects on our Planet. It seems logical then that this would affect the inhabitants, as well. The most obvious of these is the effect if the earths gravitational pull on the Oceans' tides.

The Moon's gravitational attraction is stronger on the side of the Earth closest to the Moon and weaker on the opposite side. Since the Earth, and the oceans in particular, is not perfectly rigid it is stretched out along the line toward the Moon. From our perspective on the Earth's surface we see two small bulges, one in the direction of the Moon and one directly opposite.

The effect is much stronger in the ocean water than in the solid crust so the water bulges are higher than the terrestrial bulges. And because the Earth rotates much faster than the Moon moves in its orbit, the bulges move around the Earth about once a day giving two high tides per day.

But the Earth is not completely fluid, either. The Earth's rotation carries the Earth's bulges slightly ahead of the point directly beneath the Moon. This means that the force between the Earth and the Moon is not exactly along the line between their centres. This produces a **torque** on the Earth and an accelerating force on the Moon. This slows down the Earth's rotation by about 1.5 milliseconds per century while it raises the Moon into a higher orbit by about 3.8 centimetres per year.

Because the gravitational interaction is asymmetric, it causes the Moon to rotate. It is locked in phase with its orbit so that the same side is always facing toward the Earth.

The strength of gravity depends on the distance from the source. The closer you are, the stronger the "pull" you feel. The Moon's gravity acts on the Earth; but the diameter of the Earth is large enough in relation to the distance of the Moon that the side of the Earth nearer the Moon feels the Moon's gravity significantly more strongly than the side of the Earth away from the Moon. If you could stand at the centre of the Earth you would feel the Moon's gravity somewhere between the two.

That is why there are two tidal bulges on the Earth, one on the near side, and one on the far side. Since water is more flexible than rock, we see the tidal effect strongly in the oceans of the Earth, but barely at all in the ground. However, the rock *does* bend, by as much as 30 centimetres up and down twice a day!

As it turns out, the tidal bulges do not line up exactly between the centre of the Earth and the Moon. Since the Earth rotates, the bulges are swept forward a bit along the Earth. So picture this: the bulge nearest the Moon is actually a bit ahead of the Earth-Moon line. That bulge has mass; not a lot, but some. Since it has mass, it has gravity, and that pulls on the Moon. It pulls the Moon *forward* in its orbit a bit.

This gives the Moon more orbital energy. An orbit with higher energy has a larger radius, and so as the bulge pulls the Moon forward, the Moon gets farther away from the Earth. This has been measured and is something like a few centimetres a year.

Of course, the Moon is pulling on the bulge as well. Since the Moon is "behind" the bulge, it is pulling the bulge backwards, slowing it down.

Because of friction with the rest of the Earth, this slowing of the bulge is actually slowing the rotation of the Earth! This is making the day get longer. True, the effect is small, but it is measurable, just the same.

This is also why every few years chronologists add a leap second to the year. We use atomic clocks to measure time now, and to do this, scientists needed to set these clocks to a standard time. The time chosen was 1900.

However, the Earth's rotation is decelerating at a rate of about 0.002 seconds per day per century. It's been about a century since the atomic clocks' standard time, so the Earth is slowing *relative to an atomic clock* by about 0.002 seconds per day, or about 0.7 seconds per year.

Note This does *not* mean the Earth is actually slowing its rotation by that amount; it means that a clock set by the rotating Earth loses time at that rate relative to an atomic clock. We add leap seconds to our calendar to get the two clocks aligned. **

Despite all this confusion, the Earth's rotation is in fact slowing down. Eventually, the Earth's rotation will slow down so much that the bulge will line up exactly between the centres of the Earth and the Moon. When this happens, the Moon will no longer be pulling the bulge back, and the Earth's spin will stop slowing. But when this happens, the time it takes for the Earth to rotate once will be slowed to exactly the same time it takes for the Moon to go around the Earth once!

~She Moves Me~

Humans are not separate from their environment. If the Moon influences the weather, then it affects the condition of food crops, which in turn has a direct bearing on the nutritional well-being of mankind. If lunar cycles cause changes in the behaviour of fish, birds and other animals, then again, this will affect what is available for us humans who are at the top of the food chain. There is no scientific doubt that mental health is quite dependent upon diet. In the final analysis humans are ultimately dependent upon all of those processes that scientists do believe are influenced by the Moon.

Atmospheric conditions are a real influence on human moods and energy, as well as economics. It is no coincidence that 1998, the warmest year on record, was also the second worst in history for economic damage caused by natural disasters such as hurricanes and droughts.

Each month, the Moon reminds us of its importance to life on Earth. It's waxing and waning is reflected in the behaviour of animals and plants. Many marine species have totally adapted their life functions to the tidal rhythms set by the Moon. Seeds have been shown to germinate and grow at different rates, depending on the phase of the Moon. Researchers have found that trees alternately swell and shrink with the rhythm of the tides (a pattern that incidentally explains the almanac "folklore" about cutting trees before a New Moon in order to get the wood to dry faster). If seeds, fish and trees are affected by the Moon, then why not our equally wet human brains?

Human beings are, no doubt affected by the Moon. Women especially are affected by her and their menstrual cycle is intimately linked to this celestial body. Women are connected to the moon by our blood, our hormones and our souls. The root word of menstruation, the word menses actually means lunar "month".

Not only does the moon regulate your menstrual cycle, it can also trigger ovulation and fertile times. Because your menstrual cycle controls the release of hormones in your body, this can also affect your emotions and to some degree, your behaviour.

The first step in reclaiming the gifts of our menstrual cycle is to become re-acquainted with Mother Moon in myth. The Moon is a primary female archetype travelling the great round of Birth, Maturation, Death and Rebirth each month. This is a primal fundamental cycle of the universe of which every single living thing participates.

Most of us have been taught to believe that being a cyclical creature is a primitive or inferior affair. We believe that we will be less productive, less useful or just plain stupid if we allow ourselves to follow the rhythm of our cycles.

However, there is much grace, flow and harmony to be achieved through living in a cyclic manner. Being able to recognise and use the most appropriate energy that is available to you at any given moment is in fact a far more efficient use of time and energy.

Each month a woman will experience changes in the way she perceives herself and her world in accordance to where she is in her menstrual cycle.

The moon's cycle also adds another subtle tone to her monthly experience, increasing or decreasing the intensity of the energies depending upon where the two cycles overlap.

For example if a woman is ovulating with the Full Moon, this mode of cycling gives a woman the best chance of physical fertility, great for trying to conceive children, as the full moon accentuates the time of Ovulation.

When a woman bleeds with the full moon, this mode of cycling enhances inner expression, intuition and the development of the inner, spiritual life.

As women become more aware of the different phases and how they experience them, they find it much easier to recognise and use the phase they are at and will also experience a far greater acceptance of their bodies, their menstrual cycle and their feminine nature.

Scientists have shown that every stage of our fertile years shows rhythms and patterns related to circalunar timing. The influence of sunlight seems greater than circalunar rhythms on fertility, however. Indoor life with artificial light may have prevented people from total circalunar rhythms.

~The Circadian Connection~

Scientists have shown that every stage of our fertile years shows rhythms and patterns related to circalunar timing. The influence of sunlight seems greater than circalunar rhythms on fertility, however. As well, the circadian system seems to have a tremendous impact on people's lives and behaviour. So not only does the moon impact our life, so does the earth and to a great extent, the sun does as well.

The primary rhythm is the 24 hour rotation of the Earth. A biological system for keeping track of this planetary rhythm is built in to our bodies. This is called a **circadian system.** This is from the Latin words circa and dies meaning day within.

Virtually all plants and animal from algae to human beings have this system built in to their bodies. Researchers suggest that circadian rhythms are as old as life itself and only the invention of artificial light has slowed our ability to recognize and use our circadian and consequently circalunar rhythms.

Our inborn, possible genetically programmed Circadian rhythm has several very important functions in the human body. This system prepares us for each new day, tells us when to awaken. It triggers our heart rate blood pressure and body temperature rise. As well the circadian rhythm in our body is what tells the level of the hormone cortisol *starts to increase* from its lower night time level.

The circadian system needs a cue from the environment to run smoothly. That cue is the Sun. Sunlight sets our daily biological clock. It is a zeitgeber, or a giver of time. The light from the sun triggers the zeitgeber and thus the whole process begins.

Light enters the retina of the eye. And then photic (light) signals sent by the lens and retina of the eyes are converted into hormone signals by the pineal gland. It is the pineal gland which signals the onset of puberty in humans and plays a part in the fertility rhythms of all species.

Light goes from the retina to special pathways to the hypothalamus. Researchers believe that powerful time-keepers are located in the hypothalamus.

These nerve cells called the SCN or pacemaker, which respond to light from the retina also send electrical and chemical messages to other parts of the brain and body. The pacemaker sets the pace of the body's rhythms. It keeps them coordinated with each other and with the Earths rotation. It sends information through electrical and chemical impulses to other arts of the brain. These include the pituitary gland, the pineal gland and other parts of the brain stem. These tissues in turn send hormonal messages to other parts of the body. The heart liver kidneys and intestines are all kept in time with the pacemaker by this function.

Light goes from the sun, through the retina and to the pineal gland. There the signals are changed in to chemical and electric signals and then sent to the rest of the brain and throughout the body.

In the study of biological rhythms, one of the most interesting hormones is melatonin. This hormone is secreted by the pineal gland. Melatonin is secreted rhythmically in time with the biological clock. Highest levels of melatonin are reached in the darkness and this hormone reacts directly to sunlight which suppresses its flow.

Recent studies have indicated that Melatonin influences biological rhythms by acting directly on the pacemaker within the hypothalamus gland. Some researchers suggest that the specific purpose of melatonin is to register darkness in the environment.

Since light from the sun has been shown to have such an obvious physical affect on our brains and our bodies, the reflected sunlight that the moons gives us at night must also have an effect on us as human beings. Research has demonstrated over and over again that human beings respond to circadian rhythms with biological clocks that seem to run automatically.

Countless behaviours and biological reactions depend on the rhythm of the rotation of the Earth, Sun and Moon. As well, our fertility cycles exhibit an obvious monthly rhythm. The light source that has a monthly periodicity is, of course, the Moon. Although she is quiet her influence is just as great as if not more so than her much louder brother, the sun.

In view of the fact that the zeitgeber of the human body is usually the sun, it makes sense then that the absence of the sun has some effect on the body. Given that the time of day when the sun does not shine is also the time of day (or night) when the moon is out, doesn't it stand to reason that the moon has the same effect on our body's circadian rhythms as the sun does?

~Animal Magnetism~

Could it be that the prompting motivation rests in the influence of the sun and moon which cause the ocean tides, rather than the actual tidal stages or flow which cause the changes in plant and animal behaviour and habits?

To regulate birth planning here on earth it seems logical

to use the sun as a guide. However, sea life also needs to plan such events and deep sea does not see the sun. The sea's guides are the tides and aquatic animals use the moon as their cue. Because the tides correspond with the relation of the rotations of the Earth and the moon, and these species have biological clocks that keep lunar rhythm, (circalundian) they know the appropriate time for breeding even when the moon isn't visible.

Some terrestrial animals, particularly the nocturnal ones, breed according to lunar rhythms. Those animals considered to be closest to humans have a biological clock that closely follows the cycles of the Moon. Primates have decidedly circalunar systems in all parts of the world.

Fishermen and researchers alike have discovered that the size of shellfish varies with the phase of the moon. Red crabs, mussels oysters and sea urchins are "full at full moon and "empty" at a new moon. Some people say the flavour also varies depending on the phase the moon was in when the shell fish was caught.

One convincing experiment was when Dr. Frank A. Brown, a biologist at North-western University, had some live oysters flown to his lab near Chicago. Oysters in the wild open their shells with each high tide, and Dr. Brown wanted to see if this was due to the change in ocean levels or to a force from the moon itself.

During the first week they continued to open their shells with the high tides from their ocean home. But by the second week, they had adjusted their shell-openings to when the moon was directly overhead in Chicago.

A fisherman, Knight also did a study of the moons influence on fishing. He examined approximately 200 fish catches. Over 90 percent of the fish caught were caught during the dark of the moon (new moon) when the effects of the Solunar Periods appear to be greatest. These catches were made, in fact during the actual times of the Solunar Periods.

During1935 1939 Knight made extensive studies of game birds and animals. As had been suspected, these also responded to the prompting stimulus of the Solunar Periods.

An interesting study done by a group of veterinarians in the US, has to do with the electromagnetic fields of animals. They have found that there is an electromagnetic energy field (EMF) to every organ in an animals body. This can be detected by EAV (Electro-acupuncture).

This is a system that can measure the milliamps of energy output from specific acupuncture points on the fingers and toes of the body related to each organ system. One can also photograph this EMF or Life Force (called "Chi" by the Chinese practitioners of acupuncture.) There are energy link relationships from one physical structure to another in the body; for example, the lens of the eye is linked energetically, to the organ stomach, and the cornea to the liver. Therefore, any thing that weakens the stomach or liver will cause weaknesses in the lens of the eye and to the cornea.

Because the Moon affects the gravitational pull on the earth thus affecting the electromagnetic fields, she must have a similar affect on the electromagnetic fields of the animals which inhabit this great Earth. Since the organs are affected by electromagnetic force which in turn is affected by the Moon, it is only logical to assume that the Moon would affect animals, and consequently, humans in much the same way as she affects marine life and the flora and fauna of the Earth.

~Sister Moon's Bountiful Harvest~

We all know that the Moon exerts a pull on the Earth's oceans that creates the tides, but the Earth's atmosphere also behaves like a huge ocean of air. Acting on the scattered particles in the atmosphere, the tidal influence of the Moon is the cause of cyclical variations in sky brightness, rainfall and global temperature. Scientists have also identified lunar-phase impacts on the frequency of thunderstorms, hurricanes, cloudiness and cycles of drought

Because of the correlation between the moon and the Earth's gravitational field and the weather, the Ancients developed some time honoured guidelines for planting harvesting and everything in between. By watching the phase of the Moon, farmers and ordinary folk alike could tell if the time was right for planting. They discovered long ago that it is the art of being in perfect balance and harmony with Mother Nature that will bring about a bountiful harvest.

The New Moon is a time for new beginnings and a time to increase. For example, the New Moon is a good time for planting vegetation with leaves and flowers such as herbs or annuals. This phase however was not considered a good time to plant seed plants such as beans or legumes. Cutting timber was said to be favourable during a New Moon as the effect of the moon caused the tree to expand, thus causing the wood to season better.

It was suggested that the period from the first quarter to the Full Moon was an appropriate time to plant seeded annuals. This may have been partly because of the effect of the Full Moon to draw energy down toward the Earth. This period was favourable as well for cutting one's lawn if you desired to stimulate its growth.

The time for pruning and harvesting fruit that is to be stored is from the Full Mon until the third quarter. This is also a suitable time for planting roots and bulbs or subterranean plant life.

The period from the third quarter until the New Moon has been called the "Eld of the Moon". It is said that nothing should be planted during the eld of the Moon if you expect a fruitful harvest. Instead, this is a appropriate time for weeding of the garden or crop. As well the eld of the Moon is a fitting time to harvest foods which will be canned dried or made in to preserves.

~The Governess of Growth~

There are many important factors to consider when planting and caring for a garden. Because the Lunar Lady governs growth, planting will be more productive if lunar influences are considered.

In addition to the Moon-phase astrology is also a good gauge for an assortment of agricultural activities and miscellaneous undertakings. The nature of the Zodiac sign the Moon currently in at the time a seed is sown can have either a positive or an adverse affect on planting, growth and harvest. The first day the Moon is in the sign is more intense than the second and the effects on the second day are more powerful than they will be on the third day and so forth. The influence will be greatly intensified if both the Sun and the Moon are in the same Zodiac sign.

If both the Sun and the Moon are in the same sign, the effects will be greatly intensified.

This Table gives a brief synopsis of the relationship between the Moon, the Zodiac and agriculture and growth in general.

When the Moon is in:

Aries   **Do:** Preserving, hunting, Fishing. Kill insects
           Do not: Plant.
Taurus   **Do:** Plant hardy plants, roots, leafy greens.
           Do not: Fish

Gemini	**Do:** Plant legumes. Dig beds. Preserving **Do not**: Plant
Cancer	**Do** Plant above ground & root. Irrigation. Cut hair. **Do Not**: Graft, transplant
Leo	**Do:** Weed. Dig Beds. **Do not**: Plant; Barren
Virgo	**Do:** Turn compost. Apply to Garden **Do Not**: Plant; Barren
Libra	**Do:** Plant flowers, roots & bulbs. **Do Not**: Cut hair.
Scorpio	**Do:** Plant above ground, trees shrubs, vine Transplant, Prune **Do Not**: Hunt, fish.
Sagittarius	**Do:** Plant Onions. Preserving **Do Not**: Plant, Hunt, Cut hair. Never transplant.
Capricorn	**Do:** Plant above ground or roots. Prune. Preserve. Fish. Lay foundations
Aquarius	**Do:** Plant above ground only. **Do not:** plant seeds.
Pisces	**Do:** Plant above ground, flowers, roots. **Do Not:** Transplant or prune, cut hair, fish

~Isis, Ritual and Worship~

Although many Moon Rites and Rituals have been passed down from mother to daughter for thousand of years, the Moon is still worshipped in many cultures today. Moon worship is founded on the belief that the phases of the moon and the growth and decline of plant, animal, and human life are related. In some societies food was laid out at night to absorb the rays of the moon, which were thought to have power to cure disease and prolong life Each new ritual and form of worship echoes a tradition that was held widely among the holidays of her ancient culture.

In China an authentic holiday was instituted during the Tang dynasty (A.D. 618-906) to worship the Moon, and every year on the 15th day of the eighth lunar month or during the Mid-Autumn or Harvest Moon, a "Moon Festival" takes place. During this time, it is a tradition to take to the roof-tops, mountains or any other high place to view and honour the Moon.

The Assyrians and the Chaldeans referred to the time of the Moon-god as the oldest period in the memory of the people: before other planetary gods came to dominate the world ages, the Moon was the supreme deity.

Such references are found in the inscriptions of Sargon II (ca. -720)(2) and Nabonidus (ca. -550).(3) The Babylonian Sin—the Moon—was a very ancient deity: Mount Sinai owes its name to Sin.

Among the Baganda of central Africa it was customary for a mother to bathe her newborn child by the light of the first full moon. The moon was frequently equated with wisdom and justice, as in the worship of the Egyptian god Thoth and the Mesopotamian god Sin. In general, however, the moon has been the basis for many amorous legends and some superstitions (madmen were once considered to be moonstruck, hence the term *lunatic* The Moon has also been linked with the seasonal cycle of the four Celtic fire festivals, Bride (new), Beltaine (full), and Samhain during the waning phase of Moon.

The Scottish Highlanders still celebrate the fire festivals as the 'Quarter Days,' and many Wiccans still gather to practice their herbal remedies and worship "She Who Is". In ancient times the Wiccans gathered to worship "She Who Is" during the Esbats or Full Moon celebrations. They hold rituals to pay homage to her enchanting magnificence for every season and every occasion.

Following are a few excerpts and examples of rituals in practise by Wiccans throughout the world today. If you would like a more in depth look at these rituals, your local library will have more information on this subject than I can provide here. Although these rituals are for specific days, the same ritual can be performed at a different time and day. The effects will not be as strong but you should still get the desired outcome to some degree.

Note When attempting to draw upon powers greater than yourself such as the Moon, always remember:
"An' it harm none, do what ye will." And do not forget what you send out returns to you ten fold. So be love in all you do.

From time to time, during the course of your life, you may become involved in the odd power struggle in a relationship. This can often result in the eventual break up of such a relationship. The first matter that needs to be taken care of, then is to eliminate such people from your life.

The following should be done on the last quarter of the moon. Its desired effect is to distance yourself from bragging people.

You'll need a **candle** to represent yourself. The seven day astrogical sign candles are best but if you can get one, pick a coloured candle that represents you best. You will also want to anoint this candle with your **oil.** For the other person, you will need a **blue candle** and some **oil.**

Either place a few drops of your astrological sign's oil in the seven day candle and then rub it in a clockwise direction around the lip of the candle. Light then candle and simply say : "This me and my will."

You may do the same thing to a blue seven day candle, but use a counter clockwise direction.

As well, you could write the person's name on a regular candle from top to bottom and then anoint it in a counter-clockwise direction saying: "I mean you no harm, I mean you no ill will, I create no alarm! But your ego must still!

No more bragging. Let quiet be. Of others be thinking. You clearly now see!"

Light this candle and meditate on how you want the relationship to really be. If you want the person to leave your circle just start moving the candle away from yours and say; "Good riddance to you, from here please flee. No harm to you, from you I be free."

*To Bring to you that which you desire

For this spell you will need an **Orange Candle**, something made of **hematite** and some **Coconut Oil**. If you can get a hematite necklace it is best. Write your name on the orange candle from the top down. Anoint the candle in a counter-clockwise direction with the coconut oil. Place the hematite to the right of the candle or if it's a necklace, around the candle. Light the candle and say: ***"Spirits of air and fire, Burn away the cobwebs, Eliminate the liar, Remove the fibs! Let me see clearly, What I want dearly!"***

Perform this ritual for 7 days. You can change your object of focus everyday or just stick to one topic. Blessed Be!

*New Moon Ritual

You'll need a Lavender Candle, some eucalyptus or camphor oil, sandalwood incense and nutmeg. In the the dark of the night: Anoint the candle with your oil in a counter clockwise direction and then repeat in a clockwise direction. Place it on your altar. A Silver Candlestick holder is nice but not necessary.

Tell the Moon you dedicate this candle and this ritual to her. Either sprinkle the nutmeg around the candle in a counter-clockwise direction or lay the nutmegs on the left and right of the candle, the left first. Light your candle and concentrate on the New Moon bringing you the courage and energy to know what is right and what is wrong. Light your incense from the candle flame and ask that your thoughts be carried to the Moon on its smoke.

Spend the time the incense is burning down meditating doing and knowing the right thing for the highest good. Clap out the candle and relight it every night for seven days and review your actions and thoughts of the day each night with some new incense. Carry the nutmegs with you at the end of the 7 days in your mojo or medicine bag or blow the nutmeg to the winds off your altar.

*Full Moon Ritual for Balance

You will need a single **purple candle** and your **astral candle**, some **Sage** for smudging and some **clary sage oil** if you can find it if not **sandalwood** will do in a pinch. Try to still your mind while sitting facing your altar. Your astral candle should be on the left and the purple candle on the right. Light your astral candle saying: "This is me!"
Light your purple candle saying: "This is the Universal Energy of Balance and Harmony!"
Light the Sage and begin smudging the altar and yourself. This is a process of having the smoke all around you and everything on the altar. Say: "Spirit of Sage oh so wise, Make me oh so wise. Bring me balance and harmony, Bring my world balance and harmony!"
Keep repeating that chant until you feel calm and then anoint yourself with the Clarey Sage Oil or some Sandalwood Oil if you can't get it. Say: "Spirit of the Oil surround me with balance, harmony and peace. Where ever I should wander and go, I beseech thee to follow!"
Stay at your altar until the Sage burns out and then clap the candle out thanking the spirits for their help.

The following is a portion of a chant used by Wiccans in their drawing sown the Moon Ceremony.
"Diana, queen of night
In all your beauty bright,
Shine on us here,
And with your silver beam
Unlock the gates of dream"

Before calendars were created, using the moon cycles was a way to keep track of time. The Full Moon has for thousands of years, been a time to Celebrate the Circle. Full

Moon rituals are healing rituals, magical workings, and times of growth, inspiration, and insight. At Full Moon, we celebrate fulfillment, fertility, and the bearing of fruit from our projects. Full Moon rituals range from very structured to very spontaneous. Draw down the Full Moon energy and feel the radiance!

~In Myth and Legend~

Ancient Moon lore strikes fear and awe in all who hear the tales, and casts dark shadows on the dreamers sleep. Stories of Lycanthropic metamorphosis or humans changing shape by the light of the silvery moon are plentiful as the sky. While the word Lycanthrope is derived from the Greek king Lycaon who was transformed into a wolf for playing an ill conceived trick on Zeus, the literal translation of it is to change form into that of a wolf.

Stories of Werewolves bring out the more sinister aspects of moon-lore. They can be found in cultures from around the world, but no matter where the stories originate, the full moon has always been seen as the cause.

An Eighteenth Century psychologist describes its effects: "The desire to run comes upon them. They leave their beds, jump out of a window, and plunge into a fountain, after the bath, they come out covered with dense fur, walking on all fours, and commence a raid over fields and meadows, through woods and villages, biting all beasts and human beings that come their way. At the approach of dawn, they return to the spring, plunge into it, lose their furry skins, and again regain their deserted beds."

The lore of the Moon strikes a chord deep within each of us and reaches in to our hearts and our souls. The classical images engrave subterranean notions in to our very psyches. Legends myths and song seem to perpetuate the ubiquitous Classical lore of the Mistress of the night sky and the Sister of the Sun. I have selected a few ancient tales and lore about our Mystical Goddess of the Starry sky for you to enjoy.

*The Twelve Great Paths of the Moon

A long time ago, when Father Sky took Mother Earth in his arms and mated with her, the Moon was born. As it grew bigger and bigger out there among the basket of stars, the Sun Dogs took turns biting it. Snap, snap, they went, until the moon was crescent shaped.

The ragged little Moon continued to shine brightly in the sky.

Spirit Walker, who guided all the Two-Legged and Four-Legged Creatures at this time, worried about the Moon. She told all the creatures to dance around the plaza, men with Deer, women with Corn, children with Turtles. On the Night When Red Leaves Fell, the creatures looked up. The Moon was growing bigger! It grew and grew until it had a full, happy face. But then the Sun Dogs chewed on it again and whittle it down until it was crescent shaped again.

From then on, the Two-Legged Creatures and the Four-Legged Creatures got used to the growing and the dying of the Moon. They got used to the Sun Dogs chewing on it and Father Sun casting a black shadow on its round face every once in a while.

~Legends of the Moon Goddess~

*Diana
Diana was an ancient Italian goddess of woodland. In Capua and in Aricia, a locality near Rome, there are still shrines dedicated to the old Italian goddess. Diana was the

twin sister of the god Apollo. Her father and mother were Jupiter and Latona.

Diana believed her body was very sacred, and so no man was to see her naked. One day a wandering hunter came across Diana bathing. She became very angry, and turned him into a stag. She was always surrounded by young beautiful attendants, who used to hunt with her.

*Artemis

Artemis was the twin sister of the god Apollo. Her father and mother were Zeus and Latona. Artemis was the goddess of the Moon.

Artemis and her brother Apollo had fierce tempers. According to a Greek legend, they killed most of the children of Niobe, who had insulted her mother Leto comparing favourably his children with the twins Artemis and Apollo.

*Mawu

Mawu is the supreme god of the Fon people of Abomey (Republic of Benin). Mawu, the Moon, brings cooler temperatures to the African world. She is seen as an old mother who lives in the West. Mawu has a partner called Liza. Together, they created the world. Their son, Gu, is the smith god, or divine tool. They used him to shape the universe.

The serpent Da, also helped them during creation. Mawu was the goddess of night, joy, and motherhood. Liza was the god of day, heat and strength.

*Coyolxauhqui

According to Aztec mythology Coyolxauhqui is the goddess of the Moon. Literally translated, name means "Golden Bells." She was the daughter of the Earth goddess, Coatlicue and the sister of the Sun god, Huitzilopochtli. Coyolxauhqui encouraged her four hundred sisters and brothers to kill their dishonoured mother. Coatlicue gave birth to Huitzilapotchli after a ball of feathers fell into the temple where she was sweeping and touched her. Huitzilopochtli sprang out of his mother as an adult fully armed and saver her. Huitzilopochtli cut off Coyolxauhqui's head and threw it into the sky to form the Moon.

*Soma

According to Hinduism, every part of the cosmos is seen as an accomplishment of a god. In Hindu mythology, Soma represents the god of the Moon. He rides through the sky in a chariot drawn by white horses. Soma was also the name of the elixir of immortality that only the gods can drink. The moon was thought to be the storehouse of the elixir.

When the gods drink soma, it is said that the Moon wanes because the gods are drinking away some of its properties.

*Rona

Rona was the daughter of the sea god Tangaroa. She was the Tide Controller. One night she was carrying a bucket with stream water back home to her children, when the path became dark. The Moon slipped behind the clouds making it impossible to see anything. As Rona was walking, she hit her foot against a root that was sticking out of the ground. She was so upset that she couldn't see the root; she made some unkind remarks about the Moon. The Moon heard her remarks and put a curse on the Maori people. The Moon grabbed Rona and her water bucket. Many people today see a woman with a bucket in the Moon. It is said that when Rona upsets her bucket, it rains. This Maori story symbolizes the influence of the Moon on the rain and on the waters of the Earth, and especially on the tides.

*Anningan

Anningan is the name of the Moon god of some of the Inuit people that live in Greenland. The word "Inuit" means "people." Anningan continually chases his sister, Malina, the Sun goddess, across the sky. During this chase, he forgets to eat, and he gets much thinner. This is symbolic of the phases of the moon, particularly the crescent. To satisfy his hunger, he disappears for three days each month (new moon) and then returns full (gibbous) to chase his sister all over again. Malina wants to stay far away from her bad brother. That is why they rise and set at different times.

*Tsuki-Yomi

Tsuki-Yomi was the Moon god according the oldest Japanese religion, Shinto, which means "the way of the gods." Tsuki-Yomi was born from the right eye of the primeval being Izanagi. Tsuki-Yomi initially lived in the Heavens with his sister, the Sun god, Amaterasu .

But once, Amaterasu sent her brother as her representative to the goddess of food, Uke Mochi. To celebrate, the goddess of food offered him a wonderful meal, created from her mouth and nose. Tsuki-Yomi was so disgusted that he killed her. When she learned of her brother's misdeed, she was so angry that she did see him anymore. Since then, brother and sister have lived apart; alternating in the sky and day always follows the night.

*Ix Chel

Ix Chel, the "Lady Rainbow," was the old Moon goddess in Mayan mythology. The Maya people lived around 250 AD in what is now Guatemala and the Yucatan in Mexico. Mayans associated human events with phases of the moon. Ix Chel was depicted as an old woman wearing a skirt with crossed bones, and she had a serpent in her hand. She had an assistant sky serpent, who they believed carried all of the waters of the heavens in its belly. She is often shown carrying a great jug filled with water, which she empties to send floods rainstorms to Earth. Her husband was the benevolent moon god Itzamna. Ix Chel was worshipped as the protector of weavers and women in childbirth.

*Heng-o and the Twelve Chinese Moons

In ancient times, Chinese people believed that there were

twelve Moons as there were twelve months in one year. Likewise, Chinese people believed there were ten suns as there were ten days in the Chinese week. The mother of the twelve Moons was the same of that of the ten suns. At the beginning of each month, the mother, Heng-O, washed her children in a lake at the extreme western side of the world. Then each Moon, one after the other would travel in a chariot for a month journey to reach the opposite east side of the world.

There, the Suns would begin their journey. It was believed that the Moons were made of water, and either a hare or a toad was living in each of their interiors.

*Sinn

Sinn was the Sumerian Moon god. Sumerians were living more than three thousand years ago in Mesopotamia. Today Mesopotamia is located in the territories of the states of Iraq and Kuwait. Sinn was worshipped in the city of Ur. The high priest of his temple, chosen from the royal family, was viewed as Sinn's spouse. His parents were the air god Enlil and the grain goddess Ninlil. Sinn was depicted as a "fierce young bull, thick of horns, perfect of limbs, with a beautiful bird of blue". The Moon god had several different names that referred to different phases of the Moon. The name Sinn indicated the crescent Moon, Nanna the full Moon, and Asimbabbar the beginning of each lunar cycle.

Enlil was banished by the assembly of the gods to live in the underworld. When Ninlil realized she was pregnant, she decided to follow Enlil to the world of the dead to let him witness the birth of his child. They gave their next three children to the gods so that Sin could ascend to the heavens to light the night sky.

The urge to explain and understand the world of natural phenomena cannot be seen as particularly scientific, but rather, simply human. It is well known that long before

Copernicus described his radical and revolutionary picture of a helio-centric universe that human beings, from around the world, were giving form to the origins, motions and motives of the deep sky above. Through mythic narratives of super-human heroes and anthropomorphic goddesses and gods, pre-scientific societies placed order among the cosmos.

~Rabbit and Moon Man (a Micmac Tale)~

Long ago, Rabbit was a great hunter. He lived with his grandmother in a lodge which stood deep in the Micmac forest. It was winter and Rabbit set traps and laid snares to catch game for food. He caught many small animals and birds, until one day he discovered that some mysterious being was robbing his traps. Rabbit and his grandmother became hungry. Though he visited his traps very early each morning, he always found them empty.

At first Rabbit thought that the robber might be a cunning wolverine, until one morning he found long, narrow footprints alongside his trap line. The tracks of the robber looked like moonbeams. Each morning Rabbit rose earlier and earlier, but the being of the long foot was always ahead of him and always his traps were empty.

Rabbit made a trap from a bowstring with the loop so cleverly fastened that he felt certain that he would catch the robber when it came. He took one end of the thong with him and hid himself behind a clump of bushes from which he could watch his snare. It was bright moonlight while he waited, but suddenly it became very dark as the moon disappeared. A few stars were still shining and there were no clouds in the sky, so Rabbit wondered what had happened to the moon.

Someone or something came stealthily through the trees and then Rabbit was almost blinded by a flash of bright, white light which went straight to his trap line and shone through the snare which he had set. Quick as a lightning flash, Rabbit jerked the bowstring and tightened the noose. There was a sound of struggling and the light lurched from side to side. Rabbit knew by the tugging on his string that he had caught the robber. He fastened the bowstring to a nearby sapling to hold the loop tight.

Rabbit raced back to tell his grandmother, who was a wise old woman, what had happened. She told him that he must return at once and see who or what he had caught. Rabbit, who was very frightened, wanted to wait for daylight but his grandmother said that might be too late, so he returned to his trap line.

When he came near his traps, Rabbit saw that the bright light was still there. It was so bright that it hurt his eyes. He bathed them in the icy water of a nearby brook, but still they smarted. He made big snowballs and threw them at the light, in the hope of putting it out.

As they went close to the light, he heard them sizzle and saw them melt. Next, Rabbit scooped up great paw-fulls of soft clay from the stream and made many big clay balls. He was a good shot and threw the balls with all of his force at the dancing white light. He heard them strike hard and then his prisoner shouted.

Then a strange, quivering voice asked why he had been snared and demanded that he be set free at once, because he was the man in the moon and he must be home before dawn came. His face had been spotted with clay and, when Rabbit went closer, the moon man saw him and threatened to kill him and all of his tribe if he were not released at once.

Rabbit was so terrified that he raced back to tell his grandmother about his strange captive. She too was much afraid and told Rabbit to return and release the thief immediately. Rabbit went back, and his voice shook with fear as he told the man in the moon that he would be released if he promised never to rob the snares again. To

AT THE FEET OF THE MOON

make doubly sure, Rabbit asked him to promise that he would never return to earth, and the moon man swore that he would never do so.

Rabbit could hardly see in the dazzling light, but at last he managed to gnaw through the bowstring with his teeth and the man in the moon soon disappeared in the sky, leaving a bright trail of light behind him.

Rabbit had been nearly blinded by the great light and his shoulders were badly scorched. Even today, rabbits blink as though light is too strong for their eyes; their eyelids are pink, and their eyes water if they look at a bright light. Their lips quiver, telling of Rabbit's terror.

The man in the moon has never returned to earth. When he lights the world, one can still see the marks of the clay which Rabbit threw on his face. Sometimes he disappears for a few nights, when he is trying to rub the marks of the clay balls from his face. Then the world is dark; but when the man in the moon appears again, one can see that he has never been able to clean the clay marks from his shining face.

~A Dianic Finale~

So concludes our compelling and practical exploration of the Great Goddess Luna and all her accompanying facts and literature, both evidence and lore. Because she uses her magnetism and enchantment to incite our mind to escape the limits we previously felt bound by, she will always hold a position of particular attraction to us down here on Earth.

As we gain knowledge of her majesty the Moon so too do we move toward a deeper understanding of our inner selves, and every bit of our individuality and complexity.

Much literature and prose has been dedicated to our Moon Mother and countless rituals and rites have been developed to pay homage to her universal splendour and power. As well many sacred shrines and monuments have been built to honour her majestic beauty and nearly every culture on our great planet has dedicated a calendar to follow her movement as she progress across the starry sky. Scores of Gods and Goddesses of times long passed impersonate the Moon's kind and everlasting draw on the forces of the Universe and the many life forms within it. To deny the significance of the Moon's tremendous effect on our bodies, our minds, and our lives would be damaging to the entire human race.

Since exploring the moon's powerful influence on our lives, we have demystified her ancient role in myths and rituals, and discovered how to tap in to her influence to increase our own spiritual power, and to gain inner peace, and physical and emotional strength. In so doing we have become stronger more commanding and to a great extent, additionally magnificent creatures.

For with the ebb and with the flow,
as it was, as it is, as it shall be evermore...
with the ebb and with the flow.

Printed in the United Kingdom
by Lightning Source UK Ltd.
135163UK00003B/148/A